DIVING AND SNORKELING GUIDE TO 🐠🐠🐠🐠

The Pacific Northwest

Includes **Puget Sound, San Juan Islands,** *and* **Vancouver Island**

Edward Weber

Pisces Books™
A division of Gulf Publishing Company
Houston, Texas

Publisher's note: At the time of publication of this book, all the information was determined to be as accurate as possible. However, when you use this guide, new construction may have changed land reference points, weather may have altered reef configurations, and some businesses may no longer be in operation. Your assistance in keeping future editions up-to-date will be greatly appreciated.

Also, please pay particular attention to the diver rating system in this book. Know your limits!

All photographs by Edward Weber, except where noted.

Copyright © 1993 by Gulf Publishing Company, Houston, Texas. All rights reserved. This book, or parts thereof, may not be reproduced in any form without permission of the publisher.

Pisces Books
A division of Gulf Publishing Company
P.O. Box 2608, Houston, Texas 77252-2608

Library of Congress Cataloging-in-Publication Data
Weber, Edward, 1957–
    Diving and snorkeling guide to the Pacific Northwest : includes Puget Sound, San Juan Islands, and Vancouver Islands / Edward Weber.
        p.   cm.
    Includes index.
    ISBN 1-55992-075-0
    1. Scuba diving—Washington (State)—Puget Sound Region—Guidebooks. 2. Scuba diving—British Columbia—Vancouver Island Region—Guidebooks. 3. Skin diving—Washington (State)—Puget Sound Region—Guidebooks. 4. Skin Diving—British Columbia—Vancouver Island Region—Guidebooks. 5. Puget Sound Region (Wash.)—Guidebooks. 6. Vancouver Island Region (B.C.)—Guidebooks.
    I. Title.
    GV840.S78W43   1993
    797.2'3—dc20   92-23549
                                                    CIP

Pisces Books is a trademark of Gulf Publishing Company.

Printed in Hong Kong

10 9 8 7 6 5 4 3 2 1

Table of Contents

Acknowledgments

The information in this book is the result of many hours spent underwater both exploring and taking pictures. Many people have shared not only in my experiences but also in helping me gather information and putting it all together.

I would like to thank John de Boeck of the charter boat *Clavella* for his continuous support and unparalleled knowledge of the British Columbian coast. I would also like to thank the Keffler family of Underwater Sports and my dive buddies Mike Hooley and Tony Baxter. Last but certainly not least, I thank my wife Gail for her loving support.

Finally, I dedicate this book to my father, Carl, who showed me the sea.

The languid red Irish lord makes a favorite target for underwater photographers.

How to Use This Guide

This guide will introduce you to some of the best diving sites available in the Pacific Northwest. Not every dive has been included because this book encompasses such a large geographical area. Although there are a few beach dives listed, most of the dives in this book require the use of a boat. Some of the more remote sites in northern British Columbia may best be reached with one of the charter boats listed in the Appendix.

The dive sites are separated into three distinct geographical areas: Puget Sound, the San Juan Islands in Washington State and, Vancouver Island in British Columbia. Read the dive site introduction to the area you plan to dive. It describes the difficulty of bottom terrain that may be encountered

Diving the current-swept channels in the Pacific Northwest sometimes requires a little patience. These divers relax as they wait for slack tide.

on the dive as well as the recommended skill level required to safely dive the area. The introduction will also give you safety tips and other particular diving requirements.

Because of the strong tidal currents that are generally encountered in the Pacific Northwest, the dive introduction gives a tide/current correction reference that will help you estimate the time when the current is at its slowest point. This time is called slack water. To calculate slack water at your chosen dive site, look up the daily predictions for your reference station in *Tidal Current Tables for the Pacific Coast of North America and Asia,* which is published each year by NOAA. For Campbell River and the north coast of Vancouver Island (Queen Charlotte Straits), use the *Canadian Tide and Current Tables, Vol. 6,* published by the Canadian Department of Fisheries and Oceans. Both publications are available in most marine supply stores. Then, simply apply the subordinate (Sub.) station correction in your dive introduction to the daily prediction of the reference station to calculate estimated slack water times. Note: the Canadian Current Tables list Sub. stations as "secondary ports." Detailed Sub. station or secondary port information for the northern end of Vancouver Island is not available. Use the reference station listed for these areas and watch the currents to determine slack water. Sub. stations are locations within a reference area or channel for which current data has been accumulated.

Rating System for Divers and Dive Sites

A conventional rating system for divers (novice, intermediate, advanced, etc.) is not really practical for a site-by-site basis in the Pacific Northwest. The difficulty of any site can alter dramatically with changing current and/or

The cold waters around the Pacific Northwest are prolific with marine mammals such as this Pacific whiteside dolphin.

weather conditions. The dive classifications in this book are rated for the skill level required for each site, which is defined as CLASS DEFINITION, and the geographical difficulty of bottom terrain, which is defined as OVERALL GRADE.

Class Definitions. Given in numerical scale, class definitions will help you determine your skill level based on experience. Pick out the number rating that best fits your experience level and use this number when choosing a dive site. Always rate your diving skill conservatively. This is your class definition.

Overall Grade. Given in roman numerals, the overall grade determines the technical difficulty of a dive site. This is determined by the geographical structure of a site including bottom depths and potential current. The rating of a site is always based on normal water conditions. An overall grade number is an accumulative of lower grade conditions. For example: A grade of III lists "high current." This grade would also include one or all conditions in grades I and II. The dive, for example, may be an offshore reef with considerable current exposure.

Class Definitions

LEVEL	BEGINNER			INTERMEDIATE		ADVANCED			EXPERT	
CLASS	1	2	3	4	5	6	7	8	9	10

Beginner
1. Open water SCUBA graduate.
2. Limited diving experience under "optimum" conditions.
3. Offshore reef and kelp diving experience.

Intermediate
4. One-year diving experience under various local conditions.
5. Current diving experience with current table knowledge.

Advanced
6. Strong diver with excellent buoyancy skills and deep diving experience.
7. Experience in vertical walls and strong currents.
8. Several years' experience under all local conditions.

Expert
9. Divemaster or instructor level with exceptional experience and awareness.
10. Many years' experience under all conditions including hazardous.

Divers take a break between dives at a beach in Puget Sound.

Overall Grade

    I. Basic beach and tidal diving.

    II. Reef structure with kelp, some tidal current.

    III. High current potential.

    IV. Difficult reef structures with vertical walls and overhangs.

    V. Very fast, tricky water, potentially hazardous.

NOTE: It is assumed that all divers using this guide are in decent physical condition. Remember the old adage that there are old divers and bold divers, but few old, bold divers!

Overview of Northwest Diving

Diving in the Pacific Northwest is certainly not for the meek! Although the currents and cool water temperatures may conspire to discourage you, once below these emerald-colored waters you will find the effort more than worth it.

One reason is the seascape. The spectacular diversity of marine life in the Pacific Northwest is directly related to currents that carry food in the form of microscopic plankton. These water-borne nutrients sustain hundreds of varieties of marine invertebrates and filter feeders. Because of this cold, nutrient rich water, marine inhabitants here are able to grow to legendary size.

The nutrient-rich currents sustain a diverse abundance of marine life in the Pacific Northwest. This wall in northern British Columbia is ablaze with soft corals and other invertebrates.

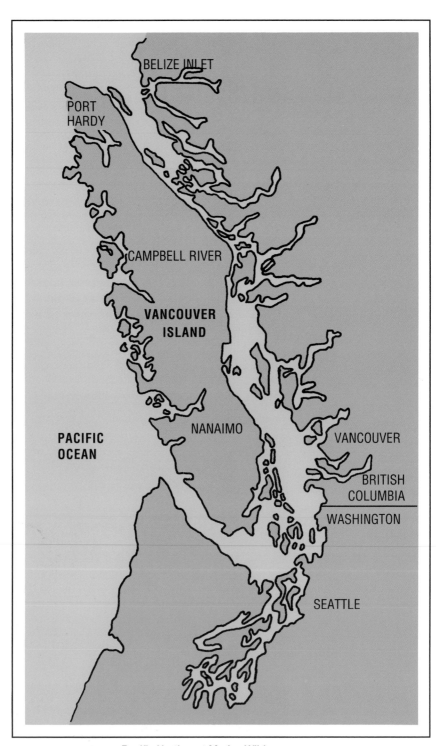

Pacific Northwest Marine Wilderness

One of the more renowned denizens of the Pacific Northwest is the giant Pacific octopus, which is the largest of its species in the world. The largest specimen ever encountered was reputed to have weighed in at over 600 pounds with an armspan of 30 feet! Fortunately, most of the octopuses that you might encounter are a little less intimidating, averaging around 40 pounds. Some of the other interesting inhabitants you will probably meet in these waters include the toothy, muppet faced wolf eel and the enormous Puget Sound king crab, which actually grows white enamel molars on the inside edges of its crusher claws. During the late winter months, male lingcod can be found nesting on white egg masses. The lingcod have a formidable set of teeth and can be very aggressive during these periods, even though they are normally docile. Care should be taken to give nesting lingcod a wide berth.

Water Conditions

Visibility. Water visibility varies dramatically from region to region and is largely influenced by season, weather, and tide. The areas along the north coast are closer to the Pacific Ocean and receive a greater flushing action than do the inland areas. Inland waterways such as Puget Sound and the Inside Passage of Georgia Straits are influenced by river runoff from

Many different marine species grow to enormous proportions in these cold waters. Off Hunt Rock, an eight-foot-long wolf eel swims up to greet a diver.

the surrounding mountains. During spring thaws and rainy weather, the runoff spills into the channels and mixes fresh water with salt water, creating a cloudy veil in the upper water column. Additionally, river and storm drain runoff during rainy weather creates muddy brown water to infiltrate the waterways, substantially decreasing visibility. High tide will often bring in clearer water, increasing visibility over a low tide.

During the spring and summer months, water-borne plankton blooms with increased sunlight. As these blooms occur, large chunks of plankton can transform water visibility to the consistency of pea soup.

Temperature. Northwest divers can describe the water temperature in one word—COLD! It averages between 45° to 50° year round. Most local divers use a drysuit, especially for winter diving, because it lends itself to better visibility. One-fourth-inch full farmer john wetsuits will generally do the job in these waters, but they tend to be a little cool during repetitive dives.

Currents. Some of the largest tidal exchanges in the world occur within the deep narrow passages of the Pacific Northwest. The area experiences two complete tidal changes per day with a potential 15-foot exchange. Proper current calculations such as those suggested in this text, will ensure both safe and exhilarating diving in the Pacific Northwest. The following information will provide some tips for safe current diving.

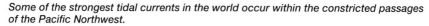

Some of the strongest tidal currents in the world occur within the constricted passages of the Pacific Northwest.

- Avoid wall diving during periods of strong currents. Potential down-drafts could be hazardous as tidal currents generally follow the bottom topography.
- Have a thorough understanding of tides and currents and learn how to plan for them.
- Use " live boat" techniques if there is current present. Divers can drift with the currents and be picked up by the boat.
- If diving from an anchored boat, start your dive against the current and return to your exit point with the current.
- Kelp will always bend in the direction of the current.
- Currents will always be stronger during periods of full or new moons.
- You generally cannot swim against any current stronger than one knot. One knot of current equals 100 feet/minute. Arrive at the site well ahead of predicted slack water and monitor the water movement to determine the best time to dive. You can throw a floating object, such as a stick, into the water and measure its time and distance to guess current speed. If the object travels more than 100 feet in one minute or less, the current is too strong to swim against.

Kelp. Bull kelp is seasonal in the Pacific Northwest. It dies off in the winter only to return in the spring and summer months. Bull kelp can grow as much as six inches per day. Kelp beds provide an interesting habitat for marine life. However, care should be taken when diving in or around kelp

Current tables produced by NOAA in the U.S. and the Department of Fisheries and Oceans in Canada provide the best information to properly calculate slack current conditions.

Current Tables vs Tide Tables

Tide tables cannot be used to estimate slack water at the diving areas in the Pacific Northwest. Tides are the vertical rise and fall of water, while tidal currents are the horizontal flow of water associated with the vertical movement. Tide tables give predictions for STAND WATER TIME, the time when the tide has reached its highest or lowest point. Current tables, on the other hand, give predictions for SLACK WATER TIME, the interval when the current has stopped flowing in one direction before it reverses its flow to another. Tidal currents in narrow channels and inlets can flow up to an hour longer than stand water time as they try to fill the lower end of the channel. Because of this time variable, divers must use current tables to calculate slack water in the Pacific Northwest.

beds to avoid entanglement. Always carry a knife as bull kelp is strong and difficult to break.

Surface kelp can also provide a few clues about your diving environment. Bull kelp will usually indicate depth as it rarely grows longer than 100 feet. It can also show the direction of the current with its floating blades waving downstream. Additionally, kelp beds are generally free from boat traffic, providing a safe place to ascend—providing care is observed to avoid entanglement.

Bull kelp is seasonal in the Pacific Northwest. ▶

Overview of Puget Sound

"There is no country in the world that possesses waters equal to these" wrote Captain George Vancouver upon his famous exploration of Puget Sound and the Pacific Northwest in 1792. Every time I strap on the aquatic armor and take that plunge into these cool northern waters, I have to agree.

Over 2,000 square miles of Puget Sound's emerald surface surround some 300 tide-washed islands, rocks, and beaches. Its sinuous arms travel inland from the Pacific Ocean and reach deep into western Washington, forming the vast inland sea of Puget Sound. Puget Sound is protected from ocean surge and swells that are generally associated with the Pacific Coast. Its shores border the two major metropolitan port cities of Seattle and Tacoma. Olympia, the Washington State Capital, rests at the edge of the tide flats on its southern shore. Although Puget Sound is only 85 miles long, it has a total coastline of over 2,700 miles, which is two and a half times that of California!

Over 2,000 square miles of Puget Sound's emerald surface surrounds a combined coastline that is two and a half times that of California.

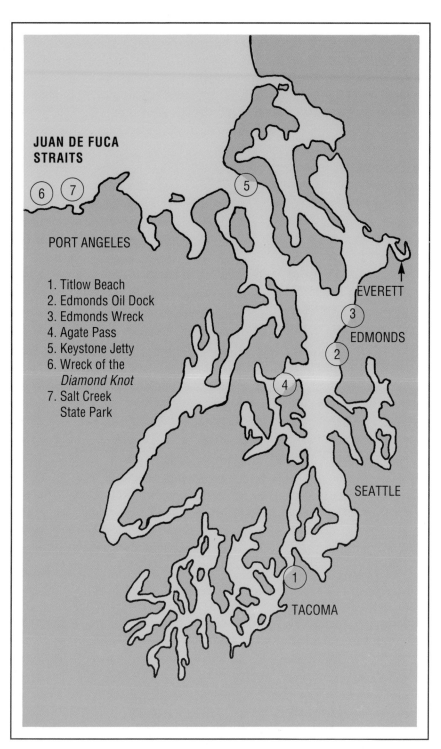

JUAN DE FUCA
STRAITS

6 7

PORT ANGELES

1. Titlow Beach
2. Edmonds Oil Dock
3. Edmonds Wreck
4. Agate Pass
5. Keystone Jetty
6. Wreck of the
   Diamond Knot
7. Salt Creek
   State Park

5

EVERETT

3

EDMONDS

2

4

SEATTLE

1

TACOMA

Puget Sound

The Olympic Mountains provide a majestic backdrop for a Washington State Ferry crossing Puget Sound.

Probably the first European the Northwest Indians ever set eyes on was Sir Francis Drake who was said to have reached the 48th parallel in 1577. The first substantiated exploration in the Pacific Northwest was done by the Spanish in the early 1700s. The British were soon to follow, and in the late 1700s, Captain Cook and Captain George Vancouver searched these waters for the fabled "Northwest Passage," which they hoped would provide a trade route to the Orient. It was Capt. Vancouver who named this inland sea for his friend, Lt. Peter Puget.

Over a century later, the Wilkes Expedition led by Commander Charles Wilkes charted and mapped these waters for the British. The influence of these early explorers can be seen by the names given by Wilkes and other explorers on modern navigational charts. Some navigational charts and soundings used today are based on information obtained by the Wilkes Expedition in the 1840s.

Skill level:	3–4
Overall grade:	II
Current correction:	Sub. station #1421 south end
Reference station:	Tacoma Narrows (NOAA)
Typical depth range:	35 feet
Visibility:	10–25 feet

Titlow Beach in southern Puget Sound is an excellent beginner or training site because of the natural back eddy that protects the small cove from the strong currents of the Tacoma Narrows. The area is the site of a deserted marina that burned several years ago and an old abandoned ferry pier. The remaining pilings and old pier structures form the main diving attraction here. Blankets of plumose anemones cover the underwater columns giving the illusion of long white hallways. Schools of silvery perch and lazy rockfish can be found lingering in the sunbeams around the pilings. This is an excellent area for snorkeling.

At 30 feet and to the south of the pier, a small ledge runs parallel to the shoreline. The ledge is undercut with several small cavities. Take a flashlight and look under these ledges as this area is one of the best in Puget Sound to spot a giant Pacific octopus.

The giant Pacific octopus found throughout the Northwest is the largest octopus species in the world. It can grow to over 15 feet in length and weigh over 100 pounds. Although sometimes spotted on the bottom, the giant octopus is shy by nature and usually prefers the sheltered safety of a lair. An octopus' den is easily located by the small piles of discarded shells he leaves at his doorstep after feeding.

Old pier structures provide an excellent shore dive in southern Puget Sound.

To get to Titlow Beach, take exit #132 Gig Harbor, Bremerton from North-bound I-5. Follow the exit ramp to the right for westbound Highway 16. Take the Jackson Avenue exit from Highway 16 and turn left onto Jackson Avenue. Turn right onto 6th Avenue and follow 6th Avenue down the hill to a small parking area at the beach.

A marine biologist retrieves a giant Pacific octopus for tagging. The largest octopus species in the world, these giants can weigh over 100 pounds!

Edmonds Oil Dock   2

Skill level: 5–6
Overall grade: III
Current correction: Sub. station #1285 Edmonds
Reference station: Admiralty Inlet (NOAA)
Typical depth range: 40–60 feet
Visibility: 15–45 feet

The Edmonds Oil Dock is a large oil pier that protrudes 200 feet off Edmonds Marina Beach. The swim out to the end of the dock is a long one and can become tiring if there is any current present. Once below however, the swim is well worth the effort. Giant red and purple tube worms transform the pilings into vertical bouquets of color. Huge sunstars, often reaching three feet across, feed along the shale bottom. The bottom under the pier is littered with an assortment of broken pilings and abandoned junk that is discarded from tankers and tugboats. These junk piles serve as homes to an assortment of wolf eels and octopus that can be discovered with a keen eye.

Although the Edmonds Oil Dock is a very popular site because of its easy access, it is best suited for intermediate to advanced divers because of the long swim and depths that can exceed 60 feet off the end of the pier. Addi-

The Edmonds Oil Dock stretches into Puget Sound, providing an excellent shore dive.

tionally, the site receives a considerable amount of wind and tide-driven currents. The Edmonds Oil Dock is a working pier, and divers should take precaution to keep away from vessels that are servicing the pier.

To get to the Edmonds Oil Dock, take exit #177, Edmonds, Kingston Ferry from I-5. Turn west onto 244th and follow signs to the Edmonds Kingston Ferry. At the light at the bottom of the hill, turn left onto Dayton Street. Follow Dayton across the railroad tracks and around a left curve where it becomes Admiral Way. Admiral Way runs through the marina and dead ends at the parking lot for the Edmonds Marina Beach. You cannot miss the oil pier on the left of the park.

A diver photographs metridium anemones along the pilings at the Edmonds Oil Dock.

Edmonds Wreck 3

Skill level:	4–5
Overall grade:	II
Current correction:	Sub. station #1285 Edmonds
Reference station:	Admiralty Inlet (NOAA)
Typical depth range:	35 feet
Visibility:	10–30 feet

The wreck at the Edmonds Underwater Park is by far the most popular dive site in Puget Sound. Few other diving areas in Puget Sound offer the unique color and diversity of marine life than does the Edmonds Wreck. The Edmonds Wreck is actually not a shipwreck but rather the remaining walls and crossribs of an old drydock. The drydock was sunk here in 1935 to act as a current buffer for the adjacent Washington State Ferry Dock.

Laying on the bottom 150 yards off Sunset Beach, the wreck is in 35 to 40 feet of water depending on the tide. The bottom is a gradual sand slope with seasonal kelp and eel grass. The wreck is in two sections that are approximately 80 feet apart. Each section is 300 feet long with 15-foot high walls and is supported by encrusted metal crossribs. They run parallel to the north side of the ferry bumper.

The Edmonds Underwater Park is one of the most popular and crowded diving areas in Puget Sound.

A diver peers through a hole in the sunken drydock at Edmonds.

Diving the Edmonds Wreck is almost magical. The walls and crossribs of the wreck are totally covered in white plumose anemones, creating the illusion of a fresh underwater snowfall. Large schools of perch and rockfish hover languidly in the kelp canopy as if waiting for something to happen. Fighting for space on the walls are bright red feather duster tube worms, pink scallops, and a variety of multi-colored nudibranchs.

The holes, nooks, and crannies along the wreck's bottom edge offer refuge for some of its more elusive occupants. With a flashlight one can spot a lingcod, cabezon, or an occasional octopus. There is a large open end that can be penetrated at the deep end of the drydock. Care should be taken on the inside because the bottom is heavily silted and there are pieces of jagged metal along the walls. Penetrating the wreck's interior is quite safe as the spaces between the crossribs offer easy access through the open ceiling.

The swim out to the wreck is a long one and depending on tide and weather conditions it can also be tiresome. Two diver-resting floats have been placed on the surface to aid tired divers. The easiest way out to the wreck is to swim to the south piling, which is located between shore and the resting floats, and follow the guide rope on the bottom to the wreck. If there is any current present on the dive, take care not to drift into the adjacent ferry slip. During periods of extreme low tides, the top of the wreck may protrude from the surface, making it a good time to snorkel.

To get to the Edmonds Wreck, take exit #177 Edmonds, Kingston Ferry from I-5. Turn west onto 244th and follow signs to the Edmonds, Kingston Ferry. At the second light, turn left onto Main Street and then turn right at the ferry dock into the parking area at Sunset Beach. There are restrooms and changing facilities in the park.

An alabaster nudibranch forages for food along the Edmonds Wreck.

Edmonds Underwater Park Regulations

The Edmonds Underwater Park is a municipal city park that was established in May 1970, making it the first designated underwater park on the west coast. The beach and underwater park are marine sanctuaries and the taking of any marine life is prohibited. The following is a list of park regulations that is enforced by the City of Edmonds.

- No boats or motors are allowed inside the park boundaries.
- All divers must dive with a buddy.
- All divers must be certified.
- All divers must wear a buoyancy compensator.
- No marine organisms may be taken from the park.

Parking lot hours are summer 6:00 A.M.—11:00 P.M., winter 6:00 A.M. —10:00 P.M.

Park rules must be observed while diving at Edmonds.

Agate Pass 4

Skill level: 5–6
Overall grade: III
Current correction: Sub. station #1305 Agate Pass — south end
Reference station: Admiralty Inlet (NOAA)
Typical depth range: 35 feet
Visibility: 10–25 feet

If diving protocol commands slack water calculations at every other dive site in this region, the opposite is true with Agate Pass. The bottom of the pass has a consistent 35-foot depth and empties into a large bay at either end, making this an excellent and safe site to drift dive. Catching a ride on underwater flight is one of the most exciting diving adventures you will ever encounter. Next to sky diving, drift diving or current running is as close as you will ever come to flying.

Narrow Agate Pass provides a wild and wooly current ride during tidal exchanges.

A giant barnacle waves its cirri through the water to net plankton in the current.

To run the current at Agate Pass, calculate for a mid-tide exchange and use a live boat to follow the diver's bubbles as they drift the mile-long pass. The dive is best done on an ebb tide when the current is running from the south end of the pass to the north. This allows divers to catch the fastest part of the ride at the beginning of the dive and gradually slow to an easy pick-up at the north end. Drop the divers mid-channel, just south of the bridge, which is the narrowest section of the pass. The pebble floor is covered with a blanket of white zoanthid anemones, and a host of filter feeders cling to a variety of large boulders. Huge lingcod and cabezon can be spotted hiding in the lee of the boulders as you fly by.

Agate Pass is a narrow channel on the west side of Puget Sound between Bainbridge Island and the Olympic Peninsula mainland. The pass connects Port Orchard with Puget Sound and receives heavy boat traffic especially in the summer months. Extreme caution should be used when drift diving the pass during periods of boat traffic. Small buoys, made out of bleach bottles and floated by each buddy team on a hand-held line, will help boat tenders keep track of the divers. As the currents slow at the north end of the pass, divers can safely ascend back to the boat, following their buoy lines to the surface.

Agate Pass is easily reached from Seattle by boat. Launch at Shilshole Marina and cross Puget Sound for five miles into Port Madison. The north end of Agate pass empties into the west side of Port Madison.

Tube worms thrive in the currents at Agate Pass.

Keystone Jetty

Skill level:	5–6
Overall grade:	III
Current correction:	Sub. station #1185 - Admiralty Head
Reference station:	Admiralty Inlet (NOAA)
Typical depth range:	To 60 feet
Visibility:	15–40 feet

The jetty that makes up the Keystone Underwater State Park on the west side of Whidbey Island is one of the most beautiful shore diving areas in Puget Sound. The 75-yard long jetty that serves as the major diving attraction here was built as a breakwater for the Keystone-Port Townsend Ferry Terminal. The huge plumose-jacketed boulders that make up the current-washed jetty provide plenty of chasms, some large enough to enter, for marine life to hide. Wolf eels, octopus, and some of the biggest lingcod you will ever see in Puget Sound can be spotted lingering on the rocky shelves and crevices near the end of the jetty.

The entire jetty is covered with hordes of white metridium anemones that crowd the rocks with giant barnacles, tubeworms, and free swimming pink scallops. Among the favorite activities at the Keystone Jetty is feeding the

The jetty at Keystone provides not only a breakwater for the Port Townsend Ferry but also an excellent man-made reef.

Plumose anemones cover the rocks in a billowy blanket at the Keystone Jetty.

gluttony kelp greenlings that eagerly congregate around divers and beg you to break open an urchin for them. The seafloor at the base of the jetty extends into a gravel bottom with seaweed and kelp during the summer months.

Heavy currents sweep the end of the jetty as all the tidal water flowing in and out of Puget Sound rushes past the Keystone area. Slack water calculations here are absolutely a must. Watch the water and enter from the beach on the south side of the jetty. Use the rocks to pull yourself along if there is any current present.

The Keystone Jetty is an underwater state park and the taking of any marine life is prohibited. The park offers a picnic area, boat ramp, and a restroom with showers and changing facilities. This is a great area to bring the family to spend a day or a weekend.

The Keystone area is located on the west side of Whidbey Island. To get there from the Seattle area, take the Mukilteo-Whidbey Island Ferry to Clinton. Once across, follow Highway 525 from the Clinton Ferry terminal for 22 miles and turn left at the signs for the Whidbey Island-Port Townsend Ferry and Fort Casey. The diving area is to the south of the ferry terminal.

Small critters, like this hermit crab, hide in the rocky crevices at Keystone.

From the north, take exit 230 for Anacortes and Whidbey Island from I-5. Follow Highway 20 west for 12 miles then turn left, following the signs for Deception Pass and Whidbey Island. Travel south on Whidbey Island for 25 miles and follow the signs for the Whidbey Island-Port Townsend Ferry.

Fort Casey State Park

The 227-acre Fort Casey State Park is an excellent area to picnic and explore after a dive at the Keystone Jetty. Fort Casey was built in 1898, on Admiralty Head, to guard the entrance to Puget Sound during the Spanish-American War. Together with Fort Ward across Admiralty Inlet at Port Townsend, and Fort Flagler to the south on Marrowstone Island, it formed what was known as the "triangle of death." Any enemy ship attempting to sail into Puget Sound would pass within range of the heavy coastal artillery cannons that were in place at these forts. Fortunately, no enemy ships ever attempted access into Puget Sound and the guns were never used. In 1950 the forts were decommissioned.

Today, Fort Casey is a Washington state park and the old gun emplacements and artillery bunkers are an interesting and fun place to explore. Bring a picnic lunch and walk the long sandy beach below the fort.

Skill level:	8–10
Overall grade:	V
Current correction:	Sub. station #1073 Angeles Point
Reference station:	Race Rocks (NOAA)
Typical depth range:	75–130 feet
Visibility:	variable

Resting on the current swept substrate off Tongue Point in the Straits of Juan de Fuca is what many consider to be the Mount Everest of northwest diving—the wreck of the *M.S. Diamond Knot.* This 326-foot freighter is a truly classic wreck dive that is accessible only a few days a year when the tide and weather conditions match favorably. The dive is best done at a slack ebb or low tide during periods of very small tidal exchanges. Additionally, this is not a dive for everyone. The combination of extreme dark depths, very strong currents, and the hazards of a shipwreck makes this a dive for the experienced advanced and instructor level divers only.

The wreck is intact, laying on her starboard side in 135 feet of water off Crescent Beach on the west side of Tongue Point. The top portion of the wreck starts in 75 feet of water. About 90 percent of the port hull was cut away during the salvage operation, leaving gaping holes in the side of the

The wreck of the 326-foot freighter Diamond Knot *is a classic wreck dive in the Straits of Juan de Fuca.*

ship. Extreme care should be observed because of loose cables and fishing line. Do not, under any circumstances, enter the hull of the ship where there is jagged metal and heavy silt because you could easily become disoriented.

Some of the biggest creatures you will ever see skulk about the dark holes of the wreck, including lingcod, wolf eels, and snapper. The wreck is encrusted with a variety of marine invertebrates that has transformed this rusting hulk into one of the most colorful shipwrecks on the West Coast.

The story of the *Diamond Knot* and the events that led to her watery grave off the Olympic Peninsula is one of the more interesting tales in the annals of northwest maritime history.

In the early morning hours of August 13, 1947, the 326-foot Coastal Freighter *M.S. Diamond Knot* was inbound for Seattle in the Strait of Juan De Fuca from Bristol Bay, Alaska. Her cargo of canned salmon represented 10 percent of the total salmon packed from southeast Alaska for that year. A heavy fog had built in the straits in the predawn hours. Suddenly, and without warning, the outbound freighter *Fenn Victory* charged out of the mist and rammed the bow of the *Diamond Knot*.

Deep water and dark holes hide many of the Diamond Knot's *denizens.*

A crimson anemone grows from the encrusted wreckage of the Diamond Knot.

The violent collision entangled the two ships and rescue tugs worked frantically to free the vessels. Once separated, it became apparent that the *Diamond Knot* had suffered a fatal blow. The *Fenn Victory* managed to return to Seattle under her own power. The plan was to tow the *Diamond Knot* eight miles to shore and beach her on Crescent Beach in an attempt to save her cargo. Unfortunately, a fierce riptide had built off Tongue Point as the outgoing and incoming tides met in a caldron of swirling water. When the foundering ship met this maelstrom, she rolled over and sank in the frigid waters off Crescent Beach. Fortunately, no lives were lost in the mishap. The 77-day salvage of the *Diamond Knot's* cargo became one of the most sensational recovery attempts in maritime history.

The wreck of the *Diamond Knot* is accessible only by boat and is best dived with one of the experienced charter operators in the area. If on your own, drive to Port Angeles on the northern edge of the Olympic Peninsula. From Port Angeles, head west on Highway 101 to the Highway 112 junction. Turn right onto Highway 112 and head west towards Neah Bay for five miles. Turn right onto Freshwater Bay Road and follow it two and a half miles to the boat launch at Freshwater Bay. Launch here and head west to Tongue Point. The wreck is approximately one-fourth mile off Tongue Point.

Because there are no surface references, use NOAA chart 18465 (Strait of Juan de Fuca—East Part) and locate the wreck with a depth sounder. Once located, hook the wreck with a grappling hook and secure an anchor to the wreck. Use the anchor line as an ascent and descent line. Carefully monitor water movement and time and depth limits. Use extreme caution on this dive!

Skill level:	6–8
Overall grade:	III
Current correction:	Sub. station #1073 Angeles Point
Reference station:	Race Rocks (NOAA)
Typical depth range:	40–50 feet
Visibility:	15–30 feet

Salt Water State Park off Tongue Point on the Olympic Peninsula is one of the few diving areas in Washington that is subject to surge and ocean swells rolling in from the Pacific. In addition, strong tidal currents sweeping down the straits make this an advanced diving area. Below, however, is one of the most spectacular diving areas in Washington.

Large black volcanic slabs lead the way past a huge kelp bed that supports a large variety of fish life. Large schools of quillback and black rockfish hover

Huge anemones like these fish-eating tealias thrive on the rocky substrate off Salt Creek State Park.

below the kelp canopy. The rocky reef along the shoreline offers several deep channels and large crevices to explore. The reef is punctuated with several sand chutes that lead into deeper water. Large lingcod and cabezon like to sit on the current-washed ledges along the reef. The abundance of these large fish is due to the fact that Salt Creek is a marine preserve and spearfishing or any marine life removal is banned.

Some of the other critters that can be found in this area include goose-neck barnacles, red-irish lords, and a selection of some of the 90 starfish varieties that are indigenous to the Pacific Northwest. For photographers, Salt Creek is a good area to find giant fish-eating tealia anemones, which often reach 15 inches in diameter. Nestled among the rocky crevices beyond the kelp bed, these large anemones secrete a stinging poison from their tentacles that paralyzes their prey. Once immobile, the anemone can then draw the victim into its mouth.

There are three diving sites along the shoreline that require a little hike from the camping area. Follow one of the trails from campsites 5, 62, and between 57 and 58, which lead down to the water's edge. There are restrooms, showers, and over 80 campsites, making this an ideal place for a weekend dive trip. The Olympic Peninsula is a great area to explore after diving, offering the only living rain forest in North America.

To get to Salt Creek State Park, drive to Port Angeles on the northern edge of the Olympic Peninsula. From Port Angeles, head west on Highway 101 to the Highway 112 junction. Turn right onto Highway 112 and head west towards Neah Bay. Follow signs to the Salt Creek Recreational Area.

The business end of the fish-eating tealia anemone makes an intriguing photo.

3

Overview of the San Juan Islands

Standing on the northern boundary of Puget Sound, you can see the islands on a clear day. They are the remaining summits of an ancient mountain range that settled into the sea millions of years ago. Today, these remaining mountain tops make up the rugged and picturesque archipelago of Washington's San Juan Islands. Although the exact number is somewhat variable with the tide, it is generally agreed that the island group consists of 172 islands, rocks, and reefs.

The islands vary in size from automobile-sized tidal rocks to Orcas Island, which unfolds to 57 square miles and rises to 2,409 feet above the surrounding straits. The narrow channels that weave these islands together,

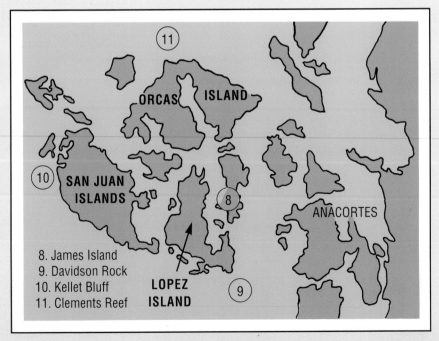

8. James Island
9. Davidson Rock
10. Kellet Bluff
11. Clements Reef

The San Juan Islands

Mt. Baker looms over the San Juan Islands. This is definitely cold water diving. (Photo by Carl Weber)

sometimes by only a few yards, average an incredible 600 feet in depth! Needless to say, tidal currents around the island can at times be fierce.

Friday Harbor on San Juan Island is the largest town in the islands. Once little more than a fishing village, Friday Harbor has evolved into a tourist mecca for travelers flocking to the islands during the summer months. Friday Harbor offers all the amenities one might expect in a town of its size. Additionally, there are several resorts, marinas, and camping grounds scattered throughout the archipelago.

The San Juan Islands are easily accessible from the Washington State Ferry Terminal in Anacortes, on the Washington mainland side. Billed as "the most scenic ride in the world," the ferry services the four major islands: Lopez, Shaw, Orcas, and San Juan. Additionally, the ferry serves Sydney on Vancouver Island.

Divers reflect on the day's adventures as sunset looms over the San Juan Islands. (Photo by Carl Weber)

The Pig War

San Juan Island played a little known role in U.S. history that almost escalated into war with the British. In the mid 1800s, the United States was involved in a boundary dispute with the British. Both sides wanted to claim the San Juan Islands as their territory. The U. S. Army occupied the south cape of San Juan Island, which is now known as American Camp, while the British held an outpost along the island's western shore called English Camp.

In the midst of the thirteen-year dispute, a Yankee homesteader named Lyman Cutler shot and killed a pig he found rooting in his vegetable garden. Unfortunately, the pig belonged to John Griffin who was the British magistrate for the island. When Griffin threatened to jail Cutler over the incident, he sought protection from the American authorities. The incident escalated into an international conflict with both sides ready to go to war over the death of the pig. Both sides wisely settled their differences, and the United States–Canadian Border was eventually designated where it now stands today.

James Island   8

Skill level:	5–6
Overall grade:	IV
Current correction:	Sub. station #1621 Fauntleroy Point
Reference station:	Rosario Strait (NOAA)
Typical depth range:	20–60+ feet
Visibility:	10–25 feet

James Island along the western boundary of Rosario Strait is an island state park with camping sites, pit toilets, and mooring buoys making it a popular destination for weekend divers. This small 113-acre island offers no ferry service and is accessed only by private boat.

Although several areas of the island's perimeter offer good diving, the best site can be found along the walls on the island's north side. The wall drops rapidly and steps down in a series of ledges and rocky fingers, eventually cascading to depths over 25 fathoms. The wall is exposed to the strong tidal currents of Rosario Strait. Use a live pick-up boat. There is some kelp during the summer months. Visibility can vary a great deal as Rosario Strait flushes a lot of silt and runoff by rivers dumping into the sea from the North Cascades Mountains.

A sharp eye is required to spot one of the beautiful clown shrimp that hide among the tentacles and base of the crimson anemone.

*Crimson anemones
thrive at James Island.*

The marine life along the walls is varied and colorful. Orange and white plumose anemones crowd the fissures in the rocks along with crimson anemones. These brilliant pink anemones play a symbiotic role with brightly hued commensal clown shrimp that live among their tentacles. Take a flashlight or a macro lens if you are a photographer and look closely at the anemone's base and tentacles for these almost translucent, tiny creatures. Rockfish, boxcrabs, and scallops are also plentiful here. Cloud sponges can be found clinging to the wall at deeper depths.

The rocky kelp beds in the cove on the west side of the island are a good spot for beginning divers who want to avoid the stronger currents on the north side.

James Island is one-fourth mile off the east side of Decatur Island and is an easy run from Anacortes in good weather. Launch from Fidalgo Head near Anacortes, and run two and a half miles west across Rosario Strait to James Island. Drop divers close to the wall on the north side and drift in the direction of the current. In the cove, anchor on the outside of the kelp beds and start your dive against the current.

Skill level:	7–8
Overall grade:	IV
Current correction:	Sub. station #1573 Colville Island
Reference station:	Rosario Strait (NOAA)
Typical depth range:	20–60+ feet
Visibility:	10–40 feet

Davidson Rock, also known as the "Lopez Pinnacle," is like a seamount in its configuration. Rising abruptly from the seafloor at 40 fathoms and standing within 10 feet of the surface, Davidson Rock is marked by a 15-foot tall concrete light marker. The top and sides of this underwater spectacle are teeming with an incredible diversity of marine life making this an absolutely beautiful dive. Tealia anemones, crimson anemones, soft coral, encrusting and finger sponge, and various other multi-colored invertebrates fight each other for space along the current-carved walls and canyons of this site.

Davidson Rock is located a half mile south of the southeast tip of Lopez Island at the west entrance to Rosario Strait. The top of the rock is heavily carved with canyons and crevices that lead to the outer edges of the rock. The edge drops over to vertical, overhanging walls to 40 fathoms. The top of the

A diver drops over an overhang at Davidson Rock.

A colorful scaley head sculpin suspiciously eyes the photographer.

rock is covered with a thick kelp canopy during the summer months. The currents are swift on the top of the rock and caution should be observed for downdrafting currents on the walls. The wall offers no bottom reference. Buoyancy, time, and depth should be closely monitored. Use a live pick-up boat. Keep an eye out for fishing lines and nets.

Originally named Entrance Rock because of its location in Rosario Strait, Davidson Rock takes its current name from Capt. George Davidson who surveyed much of the islands for the British in the 1800s.

Davidson Rock is an easy run from boat launches at Anacortes or Deception Pass. Travel west across Rosario Strait to the south point of Lopez Island and look for the concrete tower rising 15 feet off the surface. Carefully monitor the water movement and drop divers in at the tower when the current slacks. Dive in the direction of the current and drop over the walls on the south side of the rock.

Purple ochre stars congregate along the ledges at Davidson Rock.

Kellet Bluff   10

Skill level:	6–7
Overall grade:	IV
Current correction:	Sub. station #1801 Kellet Bluff
Reference station:	Admiralty Inlet (NOAA)
Typical depth range:	60+ feet
Visibility:	20–50 feet

A 200-foot high bluff off the south tip of Henry Island plummets to the shoreline and continues underwater to a depth of 45 fathoms. This geographic monolith creates an impressive vertical dive. The rock wall is undercut with numerous cracks, caves, and large overhangs. The crevice laden wall offers sanctuary to a diverse display of marine life. Anemones, seastars, Puget Sound king crab, and invertebrates of virtually every size, shape, and color shroud the rocky structure of this wall.

The bluffs along the west side of Henry Island offer some excellent diving.

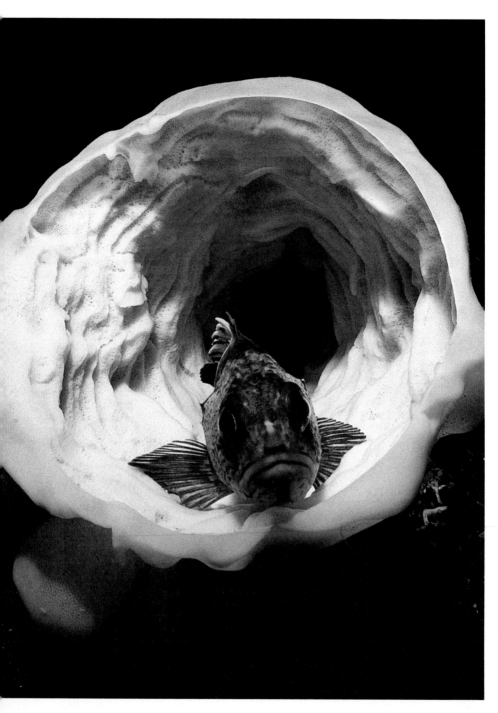

Cloud sponges can live for hundreds of years and are a favorite hiding spot for juvenile quillback rockfish.

This area is also one of the few in the San Juans that supports the soft sculptures of cloud sponges. These huge, ghostly looking clumps of yellow sponge are believed to live as long as 1,000 years. Take a flashlight and look for juvenile quillback rockfish that like to take refuge in the sculpted chambers of the sponge.

When diving near cloud sponges, use extreme caution to avoid kicking or breaking the sponges. They are very fragile and take hundreds of years to grow.

Kellet Bluff is exposed to very strong tidal currents and southerly winds blowing off the straits. The combined depths and strong currents of this site provide the ingredients for hazardous currents and possible downdrafts. Dive only at slack tide and monitor time, depth, and buoyancy. Use a live pick-up boat.

Kellet Bluff is on the south tip of Henry Island, which is off the northwest tip of San Juan Island. To get there, take the Anacortes-San Juan Ferry to Friday Harbor on San Juan Island. Drive across the island and launch at Roche Harbor. Head southwest out of Roche Harbor for two and a half miles through Mosquito Pass and around the south end of Henry Island to Kellet Bluff. A signal light on the bluff marks the entry spot. Drop divers right at the wall and drift in the direction of the current.

Speckled china rockfish like to hide in the crevices at Kellet Bluff.

Skill level:	6–7
Overall grade:	IV
Current correction:	Sub. station #1845 Sucia Island
Reference station:	Active Pass (NOAA)
Typical depth range:	30–70 feet
Visibility:	20–50 feet

From exploring serene reefscapes to gliding off innerspace walls, Clements Reef seems to have it all! Wild and windswept, Clements Reef sits a half mile off the north shore of Sucia Island on the northern periphery of the San Juan Islands. Protected as a national wildlife refuge, the series of rocks that make up the reef fall to an interesting reef structure. There are essentially two reefs running parallel with one another, creating an underwater canyon that forms a somewhat protected basin to drift through. The exposed walls on the outside of the reef drop to depths over 85 fathoms, while the walls bordering the inside edge of the reef fall to 30 fathoms.

A diver takes a closer look at a sunflower star, which is the largest species of starfish in the Pacific Northwest.

Black rockfish hover under the safety of the kelp canopy at Clements Reef.

The walls and passageways that make up this reef are teeming with marine life. Seastars of every size, shape, and color, free-swimming pectin scallops, hydrocorals, sponge clusters, and anemones decorate this underwater stage. The kelp beds on the inside of the reef provide cover for rockfish and greenlings that serve as food to the many seals that inhabit the exposed rocks of the reef.

The reef and walls have a high exposure to wind and currents. The currents can be swift and unpredictable as they upwell across the reef, while downdrafting currents can be hazardous on the walls. Dive only at slack tide and use a live pick-up boat.

Clements Reef is off the north side of Sucia Island. To get there, take the Anacortes San Juan Island Ferry to Orcas Island. Launch at West Beach Resort on the northwest side of Orcas. Head north for two and a half miles up President Channel and cross the two-mile pass between Orcas Island and Sucia Island. Follow Sucia around to the north side. Watch for waves breaking on the exposed rocks of the reefs. Drop divers near the exposed rocks and drift in the direction of the current. Monitor the water movement.

The picturesque Sucia Island group is a popular island state park that is made up of 11 small islets. The sheltered anchorages in the bays and lagoons along with several shallow reefs invite weekend boaters and divers to come and explore the 562 acres of Sucia. Facilities here include campsites, stoves, pit toilets, and mooring buoys.

The Chameleon-like red Irish lord can mutate its skin color to match its surroundings.

4

Overview of Vancouver Island

In the heart of the Pacific Northwest marine wilderness lies an imaginary boundary in the Straits of Juan de Fuca, which separates the United States from Canada. Across this border lies Vancouver Island, which stretches northward for over 300 miles, making it the largest island in western America.

Millions of years ago, Vancouver Island was connected to the present mainland of British Columbia and formed the western edge of Canada. This former land mass called Cascadia sank to the ocean floor during violent upheavals of the coast range mountains. The remaining mountain tops formed Vancouver Island and the surrounding archipelagos.

Today majestic snowcapped mountains shadow Vancouver Island in a forested land of spectacular scenery. The island's remote and rugged west coast borders the contiguous Pacific Ocean and is pockmarked with labyrinths of sounds and inlets. Deep, salt water fjords blend with a galaxy of islands to form narrow, current-charged passages along the inside parameters of the island creating one of the most pristine marine wilderness areas

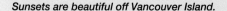

Sunsets are beautiful off Vancouver Island.

in the world. These channels are rich in marine life and serve as a playground for a diversity of marine mammals including the noble orca, beluga whales, and Pacific whiteside dolphins. Because of the abundant marine life and protection from ocean storms and surge, the inland waterways of Vancouver Island have long been a popular destination for divers. Because this area is so vast with literally thousands of miles of rugged coastline, excellent diving can be found in almost any area. The three main areas of the inside passage include (1) the Gulf Islands in the southern portion, (2) Discovery Passage at Quadra Island, and (3) the Queen Charlotte Straits along the north coast of Vancouver Island.

Canadian Gulf Islands

Geographically, the Canadian Gulf Islands are an extension of the American San Juan Islands, separated only by the imaginary international boundary. These beautiful evergreen islands are set in the inland sea along the southeast coast of Vancouver Island. They stretch for nearly 50 miles from the city of Nanaimo to the international border and are separated by a maze of intricate waterways.

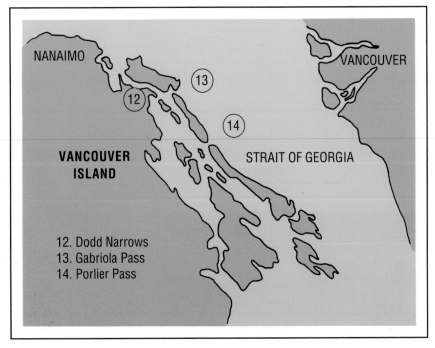

The Canadian Gulf Islands

Nanaimo on Vancouver Island is the gateway to the Canadian Gulf Islands.

Skill level:	6–7
Overall grade:	IV
Current correction:	Sub. station #1865 Dodd Narrows
Reference station:	Active Pass (NOAA)
Typical depth range:	20–60 feet
Visibility:	10–50 feet

A constricted channel that separates Mudge Island from Vancouver Island forms the fast-moving trough of Dodd Narrows. Dodd is the narrowest major pass in the Gulf Islands, and it is also the swiftest with currents that are capable of reaching speeds of ten knots on maximum exchanges. These tides have carved the rocky, limestone shoreline along Mudge Island into large craters, giving it a moon-like appearance upon first approach. Below these current etchings is one of the finest diving areas in the Gulf Islands.

One of the first things you will encounter as you drop below the surface of Dodd Narrows is the unusual vast emerald carpets of aggregating anemones that cover the rocks from the surface to about 20 feet. These genet-

Vibrant aggregating anemones clone themselves and live in genetically identical colonies along Dodd Narrows.

Red encrusting hydrocorals coat the rocky slabs at Dodd Narrows.

ically identical asexual animals clone themselves to form colonies along the rocky substrate. The anemones are fiercely competitive and fight with neighboring sub colonies who are genetically different. They inflate a stinging crown called an acrorhagi to ward off intruders from their boundaries. This behavior creates narrow ribbons of bare rock between the communities that were once thought to be the eating paths of chitons. The anemones near the surface pick up algae through photosynthesis and turn vibrant hues of green, which contrast beautifully with their lavender tips.

A little deeper, the wall breaks into a series of boulders and sandstone slabs that are shrouded in velvety red encrusting sponge. The crevices here hide a multitude of filter feeders, dahlia anemones, and octopus. Keep an eye out for congregating purple ochre starfish along the ledges. The wall eventually levels out to a shale bottom around 100 feet.

Dodd Narrows is five miles southeast of Nanaimo on Vancouver Island and connects Northcumberland Channel to Trincomali Channel on the inside of the Gulf Islands. The currents inside Dodd can be tricky as the outflowing tidal water builds in the pass and disgorges into Northcumberland

Channel, creating not only difficult diving but difficult navigating for the many commercial vessels that use the pass as well. I have seen tug operators lose control of huge log rafts in the pass, with the current pushing them up against the shoreline. Use caution when ascending and always use a live-boat when diving here.

To get to Dodd Narrows, run east out of Nanaimo around Jack Point. Then head south for three miles down Northcumberland Channel past the Harmac Pulp Mill. The shoreline will break into the narrow pass of Dodd Narrows to your right. Arrive well ahead of predicted slack water and monitor the current. Drop divers along the northeastern side of the pass along Mudge Island as the water slows. Watch and listen for boat traffic!

Purple ochre star and aggregating anemones create a spectacular sight.

Skill level:	5–6
Overall grade:	IV
Current correction:	Sub. station #1861 Gabriola Pass
Reference station:	Georgia Strait (NOAA)
Typical depth range:	20–60 feet
Visibility:	20–40 feet

The walls off the southern end of Gabriola Island form the northern periphery of Gabriola Pass and mark the spot of some of the best wall diving off Vancouver Island. Couloir-like gullies with stands of seasonal bull kelp lead

Divers gear up to dive Gabriola Pass in the Gulf Islands.

A diver photographs metridium anemones in Gabriola Pass.

the way to vertical walls that drop to a broken rock bottom around 100 feet. Portions of the walls invert to form overhangs that are thick in plumose anemones that filter nutrients from the rushing currents. Voracious purple ochre stars forage along the base of the walls and feed on barnacles and other bivalves that attach themselves to the broken rock heaps along the bottom.

Gabriola Pass is the northernmost of the three major passes that provide access to the sheltered inner islands and channels of the Gulf Island group. It courses southeast of Nanaimo between Gabriola and Valdez Islands connecting the Strait of Georgia with Northcumberland Channel. Travel south out of Nanaimo down Northcumberland Channel and follow Gabriola Island around to the pass on the island's south side. Monitor the water movement and drop divers in the pass off Gabriola's south side. Use a live pick-up boat and drift in the direction of the current.

A blood star stands on its tiptoes to distribute sperm into the current of Gabriola Pass.

Skill level:	5–7
Overall grade:	IV
Current correction:	Sub. station #1857 Porlier Pass
Reference station:	Georgia Strait (NOAA)
Typical depth range:	20–100 feet
Visibility:	20–50 feet

In the middle of the Gulf Islands and separating Valdez Island from Galiano Island is Porlier Pass, which was known as Cowichan Gap by early settlers. There is a host of excellent diving sites that can be found along the several current-swept rocky fingers that extend into the south side of the pass off Galiano Island. The most prominent of these is Race Point, which is easily identified by the lighthouse built along the shoreline at the mouth

Divers return from the rocky reefs of Porlier Pass.

of Lighthouse Bay. A reef structure extends off Race Point to a rocky pinnacle called Boscowitz Rock, which is probably the best diving in the pass.

A wall on the west side of the rock drops off to more than 100 feet in a series of cascading rock ledges. The wall is sheathed in purple encrusting hydrocorals forming a colorful backdrop behind dahlia and tealia anemones. Basket stars, soft corals, hydroids, and giant barnacles battle for space along the crowded wall. The top of the rock is a labyrinth of anemone rimmed ravines.

Another good and perhaps easier site for less experienced divers is off the most southwestern tip of the pass at Virago Point. Here a rocky shoreline drops over a succession of rocky reefs and small walls to an eventual sandy bottom around 50 feet. The walls are covered in a variety of crimson, dahlia, and plumose anemones. The rocks along the reef provide an excellent area to find octopus. The currents along Virago Point are a little kinder. This is a good area to use as an alternate to Boscowitz if the currents prove to be too fierce.

In addition to the reef diving in Porlier Pass, there is also an abundance of excellent wrecks to be explored here. There have been many shipwrecks in and around Porlier Pass as a result of the many treacherous rocks, reefs, and swift currents that plague the navigation of the pass.

A diver descends onto the colorful substrate of Boscowitz Rock in Porlier Pass.

A hermit crab scampers among bright orange tunicates on Boscowitz Rock.

One of the more renowned shipwrecks here is the 190-foot side-wheel passenger ship *Del Norte* that sank in the fog after striking Canoe Islet just outside of the pass in 1868. She lies in 85 feet of water. Today, a large pile of coal that fired her steam engine, a boiler, and the upright spokes of one of her side-wheels are all that remains of the *Del Norte*.

The 105-foot tugboat *Point Grey* is another of the shipwrecks in Porlier Pass. On February 26, 1949 she slammed into Virago Rock in the middle of the pass while towing a barge of railcars bound for Victoria. Attempts to refloat the tug failed, and she was eventually abandoned. She remained partly visible until 1963 when a strong gale rolled her off the rock and into deeper waters. Now lying upside down on a 40-foot ledge, the *Point Grey's* superstructure remains fairly intact, allowing divers to explore along the hull and swim past her huge propeller.

Most of the shipwrecks along the British Columbia coastline have been designated as national historic sites by the British Columbian government. The removal of any objects on or around the wrecksites is prohibited.

Porlier Pass can be accessed by boat from Nanaimo by traveling south down Northcumberland Channel to Pylades Channel. Continue to the southern end of Valdez Island, which opens to Porlier Pass. Drop divers near the kelp and drift in the direction of the current. Use a live pick-up boat.

Discovery Passage at Quadra Islands

The Island Highway travels north out of Nanaimo and follows the inside coast of Vancouver Island to the remote areas of the island's north end. Midway and approximately 150 miles north of Nanaimo, the highway winds

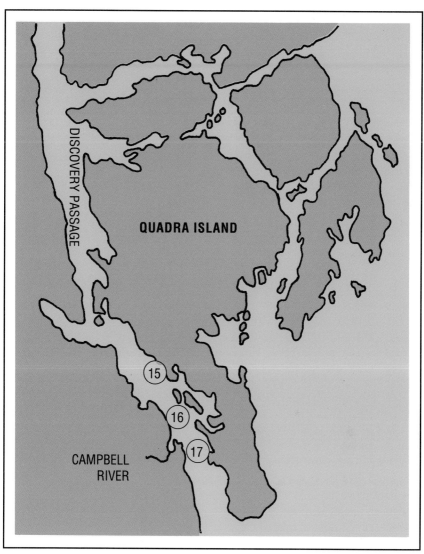

Quadra Island and Discovery Pass

through the city of Campbell River, which is at the mouth of Discovery Passage. Discovery Passage narrows from the Strait of Georgia and begins the sinuous and narrow river-like troughs that form the inside passage. These current-swept and sometimes treacherous navigational channels wind their way through narrow fjords leading to the northern reaches of Vancouver Island.

Quathiaski Cove on Quadra Island is quiet and quaint.

Discovery Passage begins this funnel as it constricts between Vancouver Island and Quadra Island rising from the Strait of Georgia. As the currents begin to build at the constriction of Discovery Passage, they create prolific communities of sealife off the shores of Quadra Island. A short ten-minute ferry ride from Campbell River will deliver you to Quathiaski Cove on Quadra Island.

The best way to visit the walls and reefs in Discovery Passage is with one of the charter operators in the area. However, if on your own, Quadra Island offers several types of accommodations as well as boat launching facilities at the Government Dock in Quathiaski Cove.

A diver prepares for an early night dive off Quadra Island in Discovery Passage.

Skill level:	5–7
Overall grade:	IV
Current correction:	Sub. station #8082 Gowlland Harbour
Reference station:	Campbell River (Can. F&O)
Typical depth range:	60+ feet
Visibility:	Variable

A massive copper-banded rock wall rises abruptly from the depths of Discovery Passage along the western shores of Quadra Island to form the Copper Cliffs. The rock wall drops away to well over 100 feet with large boulders and ledges mixing up the substrate. The wall is covered in tiny, bright orange cup corals that give the wall a coppery look. The name Copper Cliffs,

Basket stars feed in the currents of Discovery Passage by using their sinuous arms to capture small animals as they drift by.

however, is derived from the fact that there are veins of copper ore in the rocks that actually give the wall a greenish tint from the salt water corrosion.

In addition to cup corals, there are dahlia and plumose anemones, lingcod, and cloud sponges here. One of the unique species of fish readily found in this area is the tiger rockfish. This colorful red and black-banded fish is not common in other parts of the Pacific Northwest, but it is often spotted here in Discovery Passage, hiding in crevices and holes along the walls and reefs.

Copper Cliffs is located on the west side of Quadra Island and is accessible only by boat. From Quathiaski Cove, head north for three miles. Look for the large 300-foot vertical face of the Copper Cliffs just past the northern point of Gowlland Harbour.

Arrive at the site before predicted slack tide and watch the water movement. As it slows to slack, drop divers anywhere along the wall and drift in the direction of any present current. Use a live pick-up boat.

An opalescent nudibranch feeds along the rocks at the Copper Cliffs.

Skill level:	5–7
Overall grade:	IV
Current correction:	Sub. station #8082 Gowlland Harbour
Reference station:	Campbell River (Can. F&O)
Typical depth range:	60+ feet
Visibility:	Variable

Steep Island is an incredible diving area off Gowlland Harbour on Quadra Island. Exposed to the rough currents of Discovery Passage, the outer walls of this small island harbor an incredible diversity of marine life—most of it BIG! Dropping in along the northern shoreline, you wander past a tumble of broken rock in the shallows, and suddenly, a wall breaks free from the bottom and tumbles into a dark abyss.

Descending into the darkness, the wall abruptly inverts into a large overhang. As you sweep your flashlight across the void, huge bouquets of

A diver surveys a Puget Sound king crab off Steep Island.

flower-like feather duster tubeworms seem to bloom at will extending their feathery plumes into the rich current to extract both nutrition and oxygen for respiration.

At 110 feet, the wall levels out to a flat bottom that is dissected by a series of jagged crevices and sponge-covered boulders. As you settle in among the rocks, you turn and spot a small boulder that abruptly rises and scampers away! Inquisitively, you shine your light on the subject only to discover faint recognizable lines emerging from the bottom. Only then do you realize that the small walking boulder is actually a huge Puget Sound king crab!

These massive armored critters are the largest crab species in the Pacific Northwest and can attain a width of 15 inches across the carapace. They can easily blend in with the surrounding bottom with their rich purple, orange, and brownish hues. The Puget Sound king crab is usually sedentary and appears rock-like with its legs folded against its body. Once disturbed however, it can move away from apparent danger with surprising speed. The ledges and walls around Steep Island are an excellent place to discover and photograph these extraordinary crabs.

Steep Island is a small rocky island on the outside of Gowlland Harbour, just north of Quathiaski Cove. To get there, head north out of Quathiaski Cove for two miles to Steep Island. Drop divers in the shallows along the northern side of the island and drift south along the walls. Monitor the water movement and use a live pick-up boat.

Puget Sound king crabs begin life as small fiery orange crabs with prominent rhinoceros-like horns on their carapaces. As they begin to age, their color fades and their horn shrinks in size.

Skill level:	5–7
Overall grade:	III
Current correction:	Sub. station #8079 Quathiaski Cove
Reference station:	Campbell River (Can. F&O)
Typical depth range:	50+ feet
Visibility:	Variable

Richmond Reef is a difficult dive, not because of the relentless currents that pummel this offshore reef, but rather because it is difficult to locate. Richmond Reef sits 250+ yards off the northern point of Quathiaski Cove with no visible surface markers. The best way to find Richmond Reef is obviously with one of the local charter operators who frequent the site. If you are on your own, a boat with an excellent depth sounder and a little luck are all that is required.

Once located, Richmond Reef is surely one of the best diving sites in Discovery Passage. The reef rises as a rocky ridge from the seafloor to within 35 feet of the surface. Either side drops dramatically and is carved with broken fissures of marine encrusted rock. The outside drops to well over 250 feet while the inside meets the seafloor at 80 feet. The ridge is packed with marine growth. Fields of delicate strawberry anemones seem to shroud the entire reef with clusters of pink soft corals and anemones. Greedy kelp green-

Night divers assemble to descend into Discovery Passage.

Crimson anemones have long snake-like tentacles with darker veined patterns.

lings will gather around divers, anticipating an urchin handout. Keep an eye out for octopus or wolf eels in the fractured crevices along the reef.

To locate Richmond Reef, head north around the northern point of Quathiaski Cove. Travel in a zigzag pattern using a depth sounder to locate the reef that runs parallel to the shoreline at an approximate distance of 250 yards from the shore. The top of the reef is in about 35 feet of water and is washed by strong currents. Arrive well ahead of predicted slack tide and

Tiger rockfish are territorial and are often spotted hiding in the crevices of Discovery Passage.

monitor the water movement. As the current slows to slack water, drop divers on top of the reef and drift in the direction of the current, using a live pick-up boat.

Queen Charlotte Straits/North Coast

As the inside passage winds its way north, it travels through Johnstone Strait and opens into the expansive Queen Charlotte Straits off the northern coast of Vancouver Island. This area is pockmarked with a complex network of large islands, inlets, and archipelagos as it winds its way to the Pacific Ocean. This remote ocean wilderness sustains what is surely the finest cold water diving in the world.

Clean ocean water borne on the strong currents offers not only the clearest water in the Pacific Northwest but also the greatest abundance and diversity of marine life to be found in this part of the world. In addition to the lavish invertebrate life found crowding the substrate, this area is also renowned for its rich marine mammal populations. Scores of killer whales or orca pods sojourn in these channels during the summer months, feeding

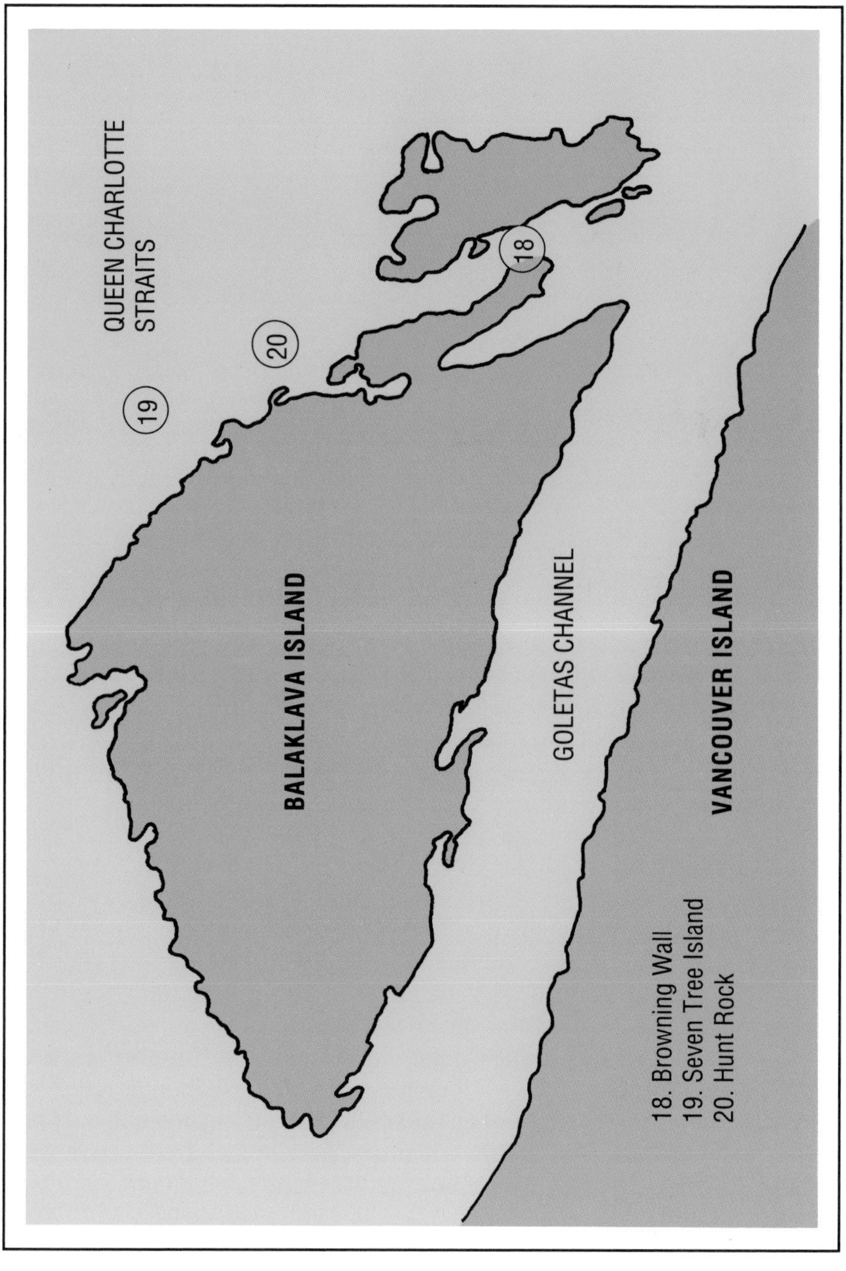

North Coast and Queen Charlotte Strait

QUEEN CHARLOTTE
STRAITS

BALAKLAVA ISLAND

GOLETAS CHANNEL

VANCOUVER ISLAND

18. Browning Wall
19. Seven Tree Island
20. Hunt Rock

Pods of resident orca whales hunt and play in the marine wilderness of the Queen Charlotte Straits.

on large salmon schools that make their way to breeding grounds along the coast. In addition, beluga, minke, and an occasional gray whale can also be spotted in these waters.

During the months of early fall, enormous pods of Pacific white-side dolphins come in from the Pacific and gambol in the clear waters off northern Vancouver Island. Numbering in the hundreds, these playful creatures have been known to converge on divers and spend an entire dive zipping around and frolicking with the divers until they are out of air.

The dive sites off the northern coast are remote and some are miles from the nearest facilities in the town of Port Hardy at the northern edge of Vancouver Island. Without a vessel that is equipped for an extended stay, the best way to enjoy this area is with one of the live-aboard charter vessels that operate out of Port Hardy from spring to fall months.

Tidal current and subordinate station information for this area is scarce and generalized at best. I have attempted to give a correction or reference station for current corrections when possible. This information will only put you in the "ball park" for slack water times. I recommend you arrive well ahead of predicted slack and monitor the water movement until the water slows to a slack tide.

The remote and current-swept passages of northern British Columbia are best dived with one of the liveaboards such as the M/V Clavella. ▶

A diver tries to capture a Pacific whiteside dolphin on film. These playful animals come in from the Pacific Ocean during the fall months and give divers quite a treat.

Browning Wall 18

Skill level:	6–7
Overall grade:	IV
Current correction:	Sub. station #1989 Boxer Point
Reference station:	Seymour Narrows (NOAA)
Typical depth range:	To 100+ feet
Visibility:	25–80 feet

Browning Pass Wall is a spectacular vertical dive off Nigei Island. This sheer rock wall drops so rapidly that you can tie your boat to tree branches along the bank and your stern will sit in over 300 feet of water! This dive is simply incredible. Beautiful branches of red soft corals rivaling any South Pacific species are patched together in a quilt between soft yellow sponge and deep purple hydrocorals.

A closer look on the wall will reveal some of the smaller and perhaps more interesting residents of Browning Wall. The decorated warbonnets, for example, are small timid little fish that like to hide in small pockets in the reef. They have large bushy projections or cirrus that grow on the top of their heads that give them a royal appearance as if they were wearing some celebrated headdress.

Another petite critter along Browning Wall is the ring-top snail. Stunning bands of purple spiral down its conical, golden yellow shell making it one of the more striking creatures on the reef. These creatures are omnivorous, feeding on kelp, hydroids, and anemones among other things.

Browning Wall drops vertically for 300 feet and the wall is broken up with a series of ledges and crevices. The wall is located off Hussar Point in Browning Pass off the east side of Nigei Island. Head north into the pass, past Hussar Point. Look for the most vertical or sheer portion of the bluff and drop divers as the current slacks. Arrive well ahead of predicted slack as the Sub. stations for this area are remote and cannot be accurately relied upon. Use a live pick-up boat.

A diver drifts among the underwater grandeur of Browning Pass. ▶

Purple ring-top snails are easily recognizable from their golden conical shells with vibrant purple bands.

A longfin sculpin rests among a clump of soft coral on Browning Wall.

Skill level:	5–6
Overall grade:	III–IV
Current correction:	Sub. station #1989 Boxer Point
Reference station:	Seymour Narrows (NOAA)
Typical depth range:	20–50+ feet
Visibility:	25–80 feet

Seven Tree Island is a small islet at the northern edge of Browning Pass and, as one might guess, it is easily identifiable by the seven pine trees that are growing on the island. The island is small enough to easily circum-

A diver climbs the dive boat ladder with Seven Tree Island in the distance.

An underwater photographer finds a cluster of crimson anemones along the wall at Seven Tree.

navigate on a single tank and most dives here involve a complete trip around. What makes this dive special is that Seven Tree is almost an example of every type of dive found in the northwest—kelp reef, wall, and sand shallow.

The southern edge of the island offers an excellent reef structure with a massive kelp bed. Huge schools of black rockfish linger in the shade of the kelp fronds while clusters of purple sea urchins forage along the reef,

A young octopus hides under a ledge at Seven Tree Island.

feeding on the kelp. Continuing around the outside of the island, the reef drops away to a vertical wall that plunges to well over 100 feet. The wall along this side is overgrown with soft corals, anemones, and tall clumps of finger sponge that extend off the wall like hands reaching out to grasp the divers. Keep a sharp eye out for chameleon-like red Irish lords that mutate their skin color to that of the surrounding substrate. These members of the sculpin family are quite lethargic, making them a favorite target for under-water photographers.

As you follow the wall around the northern edge of Seven Tree Island, you'll find it breaks up into a series of large anemone covered cracks. The bottom here rushes up to meet the wall and the bottom gradually turns to sand as you swim around the inside or west side of the island. Seapens, tube dwelling anemones, and other sand dwelling critters can be discovered in the white sandy bottom along this side.

Seven Tree is a small islet in the northern edge of Browning Pass on the west side off Nigei Island. Arrive well ahead of predicted slack as Sub. stations for this dive are remote and will not offer accurate current information. As current slacks, drop divers anywhere around the island and drift in the direction of any current. Use a live pick-up boat.

An underwater photographer gears up to photograph the wolf eels at Hunt Rock.

Skill level: 6–8
Overall grade: IV
Current correction: No Sub. station
Reference station: Alert Bay (Can. F&O)
Typical depth range: 70+ feet
Visibility: 25–100 feet

Many interesting creatures, both great and small, inhabit the rocky underwater outpost of Hunt Rock, which lies under the western edge of Gordon Channel. Hunt Rock is a pinnacle that ascends from a depth of 65 fathoms to within 20 feet of the surface and is easily spotted by the channel marker located on the rock.

Huntress playfully begs for a sea urchin handout at Hunt Rock.

The middle of the rock is coursed by a small ravine that runs the entire width of the rock. If you follow the ravine west as it begins to travel downward over the wall, you will find a small grotto at the 60-foot level. The grotto is hard to miss as the pair of large wolf eels who inhabit this prime section of aquatic real estate can give you quite a surprise. Hunter and Huntress, as this pair has been affectionately named, can be rather audacious in their approach to divers. Divers have been coming to Hunt Rock and feeding urchins to this pair of eels for years, and the two eels have become rather brazen if not insistent on collecting their stipend. If you are not used to having a seven-foot wolf eel swim up, wrap its body around you, and look into your mask, perhaps Hunt Rock is a dive you will want to avoid. Although wolf eels are somewhat ferocious looking with their bulbous upper lips and fanged, canine teeth, these two are actually quite timid.

If you can get past the wolf eel's captivation and you have a little air left in your tank, drop over the edge and check out the wall and ledges along this west side. The wall is a collage of cold water color as soft corals, encrusting sponge, and anemones all vie for space on the crowded rock. As you

Male kelp greenlings are quite vivid in their coloring, while the females are rather drab in hues of brown and yellow.

travel down the wall from the wolf eel lair, look for the large vertical fractures in the wall as it curves to the north. You can sometimes see enormous red snapper, some over 50 pounds, hiding deep in these deep chasms.

Hunt Rock is located three-fourths of a mile off Nigei Island in Gordon Channel and is approximately two miles southeast of Greeting Point. Look for the channel marker located on the rock. Hunt Rock is exposed to both strong currents, heavy weather, and ocean swells. Careful planning should be employed when diving this site. Arrive well ahead of predicted slack as there are no current Sub. stations from which to calculate an accurate current correction. When the current slacks, drop divers along the northern edge of the seasonal kelp bed and look for the canyon running the width of the rock in about 40 feet of water. Use a live pick-up boat.

Hunter peers from his den at Hunt Rock.

Skill level:	7–8
Overall grade:	V
Current correction:	Sub. station reference station
Reference station:	Nakwakto Rapids (Can. F.&O.)
Typical depth range:	30–60 feet
Visibility:	Variable

Turret Rock is a surly piece of water-carved granite and weathered pine that stands truculently against the relentless currents of Nakwakto Rapids. The tidal torrents that roar through this tiny pass are so strong that Nakwakto is listed in the *Guinness Book of World Records* as the fastest tidal current in the world. Current speeds frequently exceed 16 knots and have been recorded reaching 22 knots! Tidal currents rush on Turret Rock with such fury that the force of the water actually causes the island to shake as if it were experiencing a minor earthquake! These vibrations have inspired the nickname Tremble Rock for the small islet.

As violent as these currents can be at the peak of a tide, Turret Rock can be dived during periods of minimal tidal exchanges (neap tides) at slack tide with some careful planning and much patience. Because of the currents, this

Turret rock has been nicknamed Tremble Rock because the powerful currents of the Nakwakto Rapids actually cause it to vibrate during maximum exchanges.

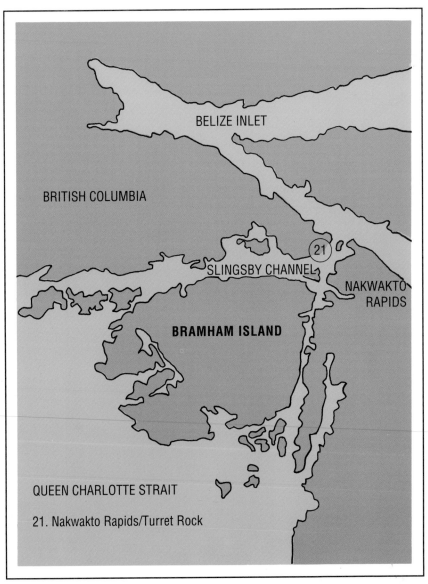

Queen Charlotte Strait and Slingsby Channel

Lustrous goose barnacles adorn the rocks around Turret Rock.

is one dive site that is best dived with one of the charter operators in the area who is familiar with Nakwakto Rapids.

The unique and almost unbelievable marine life thriving in the nutrient and oxygen rich waters around Turret Rock is well worth the endeavor

Brilliant brooding anemones protect their young by brooding them around their bases.

required to get here. Plethoric clusters of red-lipped goose barnacles cloak the rocks in an abrasive texture. Normally found intertidally in high surge zones, Nakwakto Rapids is one of the few places in the world where these barnacles can be found subtidally. Unlike their drab intertidal cousins, the goose barnacles at Turret Rock have lustrous pearly shells and vibrant red lips out of which the barnacle's cirri nets nutrients from the currents. In addition to these beautiful bivalves, flaming red brooding anemones, feather-duster tubeworms, sponge, and soft corals color the bottom like an impressionist's pallet.

The Nakwakto Rapids and Turret Rock are located at the eastern edge of Slingsby Channel between Harvell Point and Johnson Point at the entrance to Seymour Inlet. Cross the Queen Charlotte Straits and travel north along the northern edge of the Southgate Group to Schooner Channel between Bramham Island and the British Columbian mainland. Follow Schooner Channel north where it intersects with Slingsby Channel at the southern end of Nakwakto Rapids.

Arrive well ahead of predicted slack water and carefully monitor the water movement. As the current slows to slack water, drop divers along the island's lee (sheltered) bank. Divers can venture around the island as the current velocity decreases. Use caution to avoid being swept away. Slack is very short, usually less than ten minutes. As the tide changes and current velocity builds, ascend along the bottom on the island's lee side. Use a live pick-up boat.

With another adventure complete, divers head home from Nakwakto Rapids down Schooner Channel.

Appendix 1

Diver Guidelines for Protecting Fragile Marine Habitats

1. Maintain proper buoyancy control and avoid over-weighting.
2. Use correct weight belt position to stay horizontal, i.e., raise the belt above your waist to elevate your feet/fins, and move it lower toward your hips to lower them.
3. Use your tank position in the backpack as a balance weight, i.e., raise your backpack on the tank to lower your legs, and lower the backpack on the tank to raise your legs.
4. Watch for buoyancy changes during a dive trip. During the first couple of days, you'll probably breathe a little harder and need a bit more weight than the last few days.
5. Be careful about buoyancy loss at depth; the deeper you go the more your wet suit compresses, and the more buoyancy you lose.
6. Photographers must be extra careful. Cameras and equipment affect buoyancy. Changing f-stops, framing a subject, and maintaining position for a photo often conspire to prohibit the ideal "no-touch" approach on a reef. So, when you must use "holdfasts," choose them intelligently.
7. Avoid full leg kicks when working close to the bottom and when leaving a photo scene. When you inadvertently kick something, stop kicking! Seems obvious, but some divers either semi-panic or are totally oblivious when they bump something.
8. When swimming in strong currents, be extra careful about leg kicks and hand-holds.
9. Attach dangling gauges, computer consoles, and octopus regulators. They are like miniature wrecking balls to a reef.
10. Never drop boat anchors onto a reef.

Appendix 2

Dive Stores

The list below is included as a service to the reader. The list is as accurate as possible at the time of printing. This list does not constitute an endorsement of these facilities. If operators/owners wish to be included in future reprints/editions, please contact Pisces Books, P.O. Box 2608, Houston, Texas 77252-2608.

Western Washington

Underwater Sports Inc.
Seattle store:
10545 Aurora Ave. N.
Seattle, Wa. 98133
(206) 362-3310
1-800-252-7177

Bellevue store:
#59 Brierwood Center
12003 N.E. 12th
Bellevue, Wa. 98005
(206) 454-5168

Everett store:
205 E. Casino Rd.
Everett, Wa. 98201
(206) 355-3338

Tacoma store:
9608 40th S.W.
Tacoma, Wa. 98499
(206) 588-6634

Underwater Sports Inc.
Federal Way store:
34428 Pacific Hwy. S.
Federal Way, Wa. 98003
(206) 874-9387

Edmonds store:
264 Railroad Ave.
Edmonds, Wa. 98020
(206) 771-6322

Seattle Skindiving Supply
1661 Harbor Ave.
Seattle, Wa. 98116
(206) 937-2550

American Sport Diver
12630 120th Ave. N.E.
Kirkland, Wa. 98034
(206) 821-7200

Silent World Divers
13600 N.E. 20th
Bellevue, Wa. 98005
(206) 747-8842

Scuba Sports Expeditions
241 Sunset Blvd.
Renton, Wa. 98055
(206) 228-7332

Pacific Reef
7516 27th St. W.
Tacoma Wa. 98466
(206) 564-0365

Exotic Aquatics
154 Winslow Wy. E.
Bainbridge Isl., Wa. 98110
(206) 842-1980

Lighthouse Diving Centers
Seattle store:
8215 Lake City Way
Seattle, Wa. 98155
(206) 524-1633

Lynnwood store:
5421-6 196th S.W.
Lynnwood, Wa. 98036
(206) 771-2679
1-800-777-3483

Kent store:
24860 Pacific Hwy. So.
Kent, Wa. 98032
(206) 246-3337

Whidbey Island Dive Ctr.
9050-D 900th Ave. W.
Oak Harbor, Wa. 98273
(206) 675-1112

Pacific Diver
117 No. 1st. St. #5
Mt. Vernon, Wa. 98273
(206) 336-8728

Northwest Divers
Tacoma Store:
4815 North Pearl

Tacoma, Wa. 98407
(206) 752-3973

Puyallup Store:
7824 River Road
Puyallup, Wa. 98371
(206) 845-5350

Sound Dive Center
990 Sylvan Way
Bremerton, Wa. 98310
(206) 373-6141

Thunder Reef Divers
12104 N.E. Hwy. 99
Vancouver, Wa. 98686
(206) 573-8507

Anacortes Diving & Supply
2502 Commercial Ave.
Anacortes, Wa. 98221
(206) 293-2070

A&E Aquatics
29130 Pacific Hwy. So.
Federal Way, Wa. 98003
(206) 941-3115

Washington Divers
903 No. State St.
Bellingham, Wa. 98225
(206) 676-8029

Bellingham Divers
2720 W. Maplewood
Bellingham, Wa. 98225
(206) 734-1770

Blue Dolphin
1375 State Street
Marysville, Wa. 98270
(206) 653-2834

Emerald Seas Dive Ctr.
180 1st Street
Friday Harbor, Wa. 98362
(206) 378-2772

Angeles Dive & Sport
134 E. Lauridsen Blvd.
Port Angeles, Wa. 98362
(206) 452-3483

Another World Underwater Adventures
620 Auburn Way So. #L
Auburn, Wa. 98002
(206) 939-7787

Adventures Down Under
4202 Guide Meridian #103
Bellingham, Wa. 98226
(206) 676-4177

Northwest Sport Divers
8030 N.E. Bothell Way
Bothell, Wa. 98011
(206) 487-0624

Pro Divers Supply
9109 Veterans Hwy. So.
Tacoma, Wa. 98493
(206) 588-8368

British Columbia

Vancouver Area

Divers World
1523 West 3rd Ave.
Vancouver, B.C. V6J 1J8
(604) 732-1344

Adrenalin Sports
1512 Duranleau St.
Vancouver, B.C.
(604) 682-2881

Capilano Divers
1236 Marine Dr.
Vancouver, B.C. V7P 1T2
(604) 986-0302

Diving Locker
2745 West 4th
Vancouver, B.C. V6K 1P9
(604) 736-2681

Rowand's Reef
7011 Elmbridge Wy. #172
Richmond, B.C. V7C 4V6
(604) 273-0304

Dive & Sea Sports Ltd.
825 McBride Blvd.
New Westminster, B.C. V3L 5B5
(604) 524-1188

Nanaimo Area

Seafun Divers Ltd.
300 Terminal Ave.

Nanaimo B.C. V9R 5C6
(604) 754-4813

Sundown Diving
610 Comox Road
Nanaimo, B.C. V9R 3J3
(604) 753-1880

Campbell River Area

Seafun Divers Ltd.
1761 Island Hwy.
Campbell River, B.C. V9R 5C6
(604) 287-3622

Beaver Aquatics
760 Island Hwy.
Campbell River, B.C. V9W 2C3

Port Hardy Area

North Island Divers
Box 1674
Port Hardy, B.C. V0N 2P0
(604) 949-2664

Appendix 3

Charter Operators

Washington

Mystic Sea Charters
Route 2, Box 3026
Lopez Island, Wa. 98261
(206) 468-2032

Mainstay Charters
P.O. Box 1775
Friday Harbor, Wa. 98250
(206) 378-7160
FAX (206) 378-5473

Starfire Charters
849 N.E. 130th
Seattle, Wa.
(206) 364-9858

Discovery Charters
P.O. Box 636
Anacortes, Wa. 98221
(206) 293-4248

Whidbey Island Divers
9050-D 900th Ave. W.
Oak Harbor, Wa. 98273
(206) 675-1112

Washington Divers
903 No. State St.
Bellingham, Wa. 98273
(206) 676-8029

British Columbia

Clavella Adventures
Box 866 Station A
Nanaimo, B.C. V9R 5N2
office (604) 753-3751
vessel (604) 949-4014
FAX (604) 755-4014

Exta-Sea Charters Ltd.
Box 1058
Nanaimo, B.C. V9R 5Z2
(604) 756-0544
FAX (604) 758-4897

Abyssal Diving Charters
Box 421 Quathiaski Cove
Quadra Island, B.C. V9P 1N0
(604) 285-3724

God's Pocket Resort
Box 471
Port Hardy, B.C. V0N 2P0
(604) 949-9221

A male kelp greenling swims away from a colorful wall in British Columbia.

Index